In Their Own Voices

Kids on Divorce and Why Dad Matters

Part of The Present Dad Series

Brandon Antoni

Next Chapter Imprint

ISBN (Paperback): 978-1-969552-08-3

ISBN (eBook): 978-1-969552-09-0

Published by Next Chapter Imprint

Printed in the United States of America

First Edition

The Present Dad Series — Book 3 of 5 A note on the stories in this book:

The stories are composites — created to reflect the real emotions, experiences, and language of children navigating divorce. While no individual child was interviewed, every scenario is rooted in common themes documented by family therapists, parenting researchers, and the lived experiences of divorced fathers.

The children in this book are fictional characters. Their names, details, and scenarios are invented. No story represents a specific real child or family. The intent is to capture truth through story, not to document actual events.

For my son and my daughter — this book began because I wanted to understand your world, not just my own. Every word in these pages exists because you deserve a father who listens as deeply as he loves.

And for every child of divorce who has ever felt caught in the middle, unheard, or unsure whether it was okay to say what they really felt: your voice matters. It always has.

A Note to Kids

If you picked up this book — or if your dad is reading it and you're curious what's inside — I want to say something directly to you before you go any further.

The kids in these pages are made up. Their names, their schools, their stuffed animals, their specific feelings about pizza night and Christmas morning — all invented. But here's the thing: even though the characters aren't real, everything they feel is real. I know that because those feelings are the same ones that kids across the country have shared with counselors, therapists, teachers, and dads who were finally paying attention.

Which means if you read something in one of these stories and think, that's exactly how I feel — you're right. And you're not alone in feeling it.

You are not alone.

Divorce is hard. It doesn't always make sense. And it is completely okay to have feelings about it that are big, complicated, or hard to name. Those feelings don't make you broken. They make you human.

One more thing: if you read something here and want to share it with your dad — go ahead. That's part of why this book exists. Your dad loves you, even when things are complicated between the adults. And he's trying to understand what your life feels like from the inside.

Give him a chance to hear you. And if he's already listening — you're lucky. So is he.

Introduction

Why This Book Exists

I want to tell you what this book isn't before I tell you what it is.

It isn't a clinical study. It isn't a guilt trip. It isn't a list of everything you've done wrong as a divorced dad, handed to you wrapped in the language of child psychology. There are plenty of those already.

They're often well-intentioned and genuinely useful, and they also have a way of leaving a dad feeling worse about himself without actually changing what he does on a Tuesday afternoon.

This book is something different.

It started with a simple, uncomfortable question that I kept coming back to in those first years after my own divorce: What is my kid actually experiencing right now? Not what the parenting books said my kid was probably experiencing. Not what the custody agreement implied about their schedule and therefore their emotional state. What were they actually thinking and feeling and carrying around — in the minivan, at the dinner table, at school on Monday morning after a transition weekend?

I didn't always know. And not knowing felt like a failure of a specific kind — not the logistical failures (I was getting better at those), but a failure of presence. I was showing up in body and not always in understanding.

This book is the answer I went looking for.

The children you'll meet in these pages are fictional. Their stories are composites — created to reflect the real emotions, experiences, and language of children navigating divorce. While no individual child was interviewed, every scenario is rooted in common themes documented by family therapists, parenting researchers, and the lived experiences of divorced fathers. I made the choice to use composite fictional characters deliberately, and I want to explain why: it allowed me to draw from the full breadth of what children experience — across ages, family structures, custody arrangements, and cultural backgrounds — without collapsing everything into one "representative" story that would inevitably represent no one accurately. It also protects privacy.

Real children navigating real divorces don't need their pain on display. What they need is for their dads to understand it.

So: the characters are fictional. The feelings are real. Every word a child speaks in this book is rooted in something true.

Here's how the book works. Each chapter opens with a brief frame, then moves into four to seven short stories narrated by children of different ages. After the stories, I show up in the "Dad Insight" section — as myself, speaking directly to you — to translate what we just heard into something actionable. What does this mean for how you handle the next custody pickup? What does it mean for how you set up your apartment, or handle the holidays, or respond when your kid goes quiet?

Each chapter also ends with Key Reminders (three principles worth keeping), Reflection Questions (specific prompts worth sitting with, or taking into The Present Dad Workbook for deeper work), and a closing paragraph to let the chapter land.

You can read straight through or jump to the chapter most relevant to where you are right now. There's no wrong way in.

A word about where this fits in The Present Dad Series: if you've already read The Present Dad (Book 1) and The Present Dad Workbook (Book 2), you have the foundation — the practical tools, the framework, the self-examination. This book goes one layer deeper. It's about what's happening on the other side of the kitchen counter while you flip the Saturday pancakes. It's about what your child is thinking while you're thinking about how to be a better dad. If you haven't read Books 1 and 2, that's okay — this book stands on its own. But if you want to take what you read here further, the Workbook is where these Reflection Questions have a home.

Books 4 and 5 in the series — The Dating Dad and The Blended Dad:

Shepherding Two Families into One — carry the journey forward into new terrain. But this book sits at the center of the series for a reason: before you can navigate what comes next, you need to understand what your child is already carrying.

You picked this book up. That's not nothing. That's actually the beginning of something.

Let's go. — Brandon Antoni Queen Creek, Arizona

CHAPTER 1

Two Homes, One Childhood

There's a particular image that lives in my mind when I think about what kids carry through divorce: a child with a backpack, standing at the threshold between two doors. Inside that backpack — the literal one and the figurative one — is everything they need to belong somewhere. A stuffed animal. A charger. A library book that was supposed to go back days ago. The particular sweatshirt. And underneath all of that, invisible and heavy: the need to feel like they've arrived somewhere real. Not a stop. Not a visit. Home.

Kids are resilient — we say that a lot, and it's true. They adapt to two-home life faster than most adults expect. But adaptation isn't the same thing as comfort, and comfort doesn't happen automatically. It requires effort from the adults in the equation. Specifically, it requires effort from you. This chapter is about what that looks like — from the kids who are living it.

The children in this chapter — and throughout this book — are composite characters. Their feelings are real. Their names and stories are invented. For more on how and why these stories were created, see the Introduction.

• • •

Maya, age 9

I have two of some things now. Two toothbrushes — one at Mom's and one at Dad's. Two sets of pajamas. Two hair ties in two different bathroom drawers. Dad figured that out after the third time I cried because I forgot something.

The thing that got me wasn't the big stuff. It was Bunny.

Bunny is this stuffed rabbit I've had since I was four. She's gray and kind of flat now because I sleep with her every night and she's been washed so many times. I don't actually need her to fall asleep anymore — I just like knowing she's there. But one Sunday night at Dad's, when it was time for bed and we were doing the usual routine, I realized Bunny was at Mom's. I had this sinking feeling, right in my stomach.

Not a big dramatic feeling. Just a slow, quiet awful feeling.

I told Dad, and he said, "I know that's hard, bug. Do you want to call Mom?" But Mom was already asleep and I didn't want to wake her, and I didn't want Dad to feel bad, so I just said it was fine and got in bed without Bunny.

But it wasn't fine. I lay there for a long time, staring at the ceiling of Dad's room — because I was in his room that night, in the big bed — and I thought about how I always had something missing. Even when everything was okay, there was always some little piece of me somewhere else.

A few weeks after that, Dad came home from Target with a bag. Inside was this small stuffed rabbit — a different one, lighter colored, with longer ears. He put it on my pillow and said, "This one lives at my house. Bunny can stay at Mom's. You don't have to choose."

I cried a little. Good cried, not bad cried. I named the new one Cotton.

I still miss Bunny sometimes. But it helped knowing I didn't have to sleep in a house without any piece of me in it.

• • •

Jonah, age 11

Dad's apartment smelled like paint when we first got there. Not bad paint — fresh paint. Like everything had been cleaned and was waiting for something to happen. The walls were white. There was a couch and a TV and a kitchen table and that was mostly it. Not in a sad way — more like a hotel, except a hotel usually has more pictures.

My room had a bed and a dresser. The dresser was empty because my clothes lived at Mom's house, or at least most of them did. Dad had bought me some new stuff, which was nice, but none of it was my stuff.

My baseball posters, my trophy from the season-ending tournament, my Lego Technic sets — those were still in my old room at the house we used to all live in together, which was now just Mom's house.

I felt weird in that apartment for a few weeks. I didn't say anything about it because Dad was clearly trying really hard and I didn't want to make it worse. But it felt temporary. Like I was staying somewhere until the real situation was figured out.

Then one Saturday, Dad said, "I think we should do something about these walls." He drove me to the store and told me to pick whatever I wanted. I got three baseball posters and a poster of the solar system — I've always liked space — and when we got home, he let me decide where they went. I held them up and he held the tape measure and we moved them around until it looked right.

It took maybe two hours. When we were done, I stood in the doorway and looked at it and it felt different. Not like home-home. But like mine.

Like the room was starting to know me.

He also let me leave my Lego sets out on the shelf, even the half-built ones. At Mom's we had a rule: put them away or they get knocked over.

At Dad's, the shelf is just mine. The Lego sits there all week whether I'm there or not, waiting.

I think that was the part that mattered most — that things stayed where I left them.

• • •

Priya, age 8

Every Friday at Dad's, we get pizza and watch a movie.

It started after they first split up. That first Friday was strange — I remember sitting at the kitchen table and not knowing what we were doing for dinner, and Dad looked like he wasn't sure either. So he asked me what I wanted, and I said pizza, and he called the place around the corner. We got half cheese and half pepperoni and ate it on the couch watching Moana, which I had already seen four times.

That might not sound like a big deal. But the next Friday, he did it again. And the Friday after that. And the one after that.

Now it's been almost two years and we have not missed a Friday. Even when I was sick and I got ginger ale instead of pizza. Even when Dad had a work thing run late and we didn't start the movie until nine-thirty.

Even when we argued earlier in the day about something I can't even remember — we still had Friday.

I know some kids want every day to be an adventure. And some days we do something special, like go to the trampoline park or drive up to see the mountains. But mostly what I want is just to know what's going to happen. When I'm at school on Friday and somebody asks what I'm doing this weekend, I say, "Pizza at my dad's." Like it's a given. Like it's not something that could be taken away.

That's actually what I like best about it. That it's just what we do.

• • •

Eli, age 4

(told in simple language, from memory) Daddy has a blanket on my bed that is blue and soft. Softer than the blanket at Mommy's. When I get to Daddy's house I go get the blanket first thing, before I even take my shoes off.

Daddy has a dog pillow on my bed too. The dog pillow is named Blue. Blue doesn't come to Mommy's house. Blue lives at Daddy's and waits for me.

Daddy smells like his soap. I don't know what kind it is but it smells like Daddy. When I wake up in the morning and Daddy comes in he smells like that and I know it's morning at Daddy's.

There's a drawer in the kitchen that has my fruit snacks in it. The ones with the sharks. Daddy buys them and puts them in the drawer and they're mine. Mommy doesn't buy those ones.

Sometimes I forget and I think I'm at Mommy's when I wake up and I feel confused. Then I smell the soap and I see Blue on the pillow and I feel the blue blanket and I know. I'm at Daddy's. It's okay.

Daddy's house smells like Daddy. That's my favorite part.

• • •

Destiny, age 13

My dad lives in Phoenix. We live — my mom and me and my little brothers — in Chicago. So our schedule isn't a week-on, week-off situation. It's summers and winter break and some spring breaks, which sounds like a lot until you count the days and realize I spend maybe eleven weeks a year with my dad. Eleven weeks out of fifty-two.

For the first two summers, I felt like a visitor in his city. He'd pick me up from the airport and we'd do fun things — museums, hiking, a Diamondbacks game — and it was always fun, but it felt like a long vacation, not like being somewhere I belonged. His apartment was nice and clean and smelled like a candle. I slept in the guest room, which was decorated with generic stuff — a painting of mountains, a gray comforter. It could have been anyone's room.

I didn't say anything to him about it. I was thirteen. I didn't have the words.

Then the summer I turned fourteen, I got there and something was different. The guest room had a bulletin board on the wall with some of my photos on it — pictures he'd printed from my Instagram, which felt weird at first and then really sweet. There was a small succulent on the dresser with a tag that said Destiny's plant — water me Sundays.

And in the closet, there was a clear bin on the floor with a label in Dad's handwriting: D's stuff (do not move).

I went and found him in the kitchen and I just kind of stood there for a second.

He said, "I want it to feel like yours. Even when you're not here."

I didn't cry in front of him. But later that night, when I was in the room — my room — I thought about that bin on the closet floor and about how he had labeled it. How he had done that before I arrived, when I wasn't even there yet. Like he'd been thinking about me in the space before I showed up.

He also gave me a drawer in the kitchen for my specific snacks. And a key to the apartment on a keychain with my name on it. I've never needed the key — one of us is always home — but I have it on my lanyard with my school ID.

I carry it every day.

That's what belonging feels like. Not just being welcomed when you arrive. Being expected when you're still on the way.

Pull Quotes "It helped knowing I didn't have to sleep in a house without any piece of me in it." — Maya, 9 "It started feeling like mine. Like the room was starting to know me."* — Jonah, 11 "He said, 'I want it to feel like yours.' I carry that key on my lanyard every day."* — Destiny, 13

Dad Insight

I remember standing in my new place — the first place that was just mine after the divorce — and thinking it looked fine. Clean.

Functional. Like a good apartment. What I didn't think about until much later was what it looked like to a nine-year-old walking in for the first time and trying to locate herself in it. There was no version of her in that space yet. I had to build that, and building it took more intention than I expected.

Here's the truth about a house versus a home: a house is a structure. A home is a feeling. And the feeling doesn't come from the square footage or the neighborhood or how new the appliances are. It comes from the specific, accumulated sense that this place expects me. That I belong here. That if I left something on the shelf last week, it's still on the shelf.

The first thing to understand is that kids often won't tell you when they don't feel at home. They'll say "it's fine" because they love you and they can see you're trying and they don't want to add to whatever you're already carrying. Don't take "it's fine" as a status report. Take it as a starting point. Ask specific questions: Does your room feel like yours? Is there anything you wish you had here that you don't? What's the one thing that would make this place feel more like home?

Then listen without defending. This isn't about your effort — it's about their experience.

The practical moves are simpler than you might think. Duplicate the essentials. Not everything — that's expensive and impractical — but the things that carry real emotional weight. Bunny, the particular shampoo, the brand of cereal. A second set of the pajamas they actually wear. The investment is small; the signal it sends is enormous: I thought about you before you got here.

Let kids personalize their space. Posters, a shelf for their stuff, a hook by the door for their backpack. Let them decide where things go.

Resist the urge to redecorate constantly or keep things pristine. A room that looks like it's waiting to be photographed doesn't feel lived-in.

A room with a half-built Lego set on the shelf feels like someone's room.

Build routines, and protect them. Priya didn't need the pizza and the movie to be the best night of her week. She needed them to be dependable. The content matters less than the consistency. What is the equivalent of Friday pizza at your house? If you don't have one yet, this week is a good time to start. It doesn't have to be elaborate.

Pancakes every Saturday morning. A walk after dinner. A TV show you watch together. The specific ritual is almost beside the point — what matters is that it's yours, it's consistent, and your kid can bank on it.

For long-distance dads: the challenge is compressing belonging into shorter, more intense stretches. The key is making sure your child's fingerprints are on your space even when they're not there. A photo on the fridge. Their name on something in the kitchen. A designated space — a drawer, a closet bin, a hook — that has no other purpose than to hold their things. These are signals that you think about them when they're gone. That's not nothing. That's everything.

One more thing: be aware of the "vacation dad" trap. When your kid is only with you for summers or long breaks, the instinct is to fill every day with adventures. Trips, outings, restaurants, experiences. That's wonderful in moderation, but kids don't build a sense of home through adventure. They build it through ordinary days. Make sure there are some boring evenings in the rotation — nights when you're making dinner and they're on the couch reading and nothing in particular is happening. Those nights are not wasted. Those nights are the architecture of home.

Finally: arrival rituals matter. The transition between homes is a real emotional event for kids, even when they seem fine. A small, consistent ritual when they arrive at your door — the same greeting, the same snack on the counter, even just the same lamp on in the entryway — helps them shift gears mentally. You're not just opening a door.

You're letting them know they've arrived somewhere that's been waiting for them.

Key Reminders

- A home is made, not inherited. You build it with routines, with permanence, with small acts that say: you belong here.
- Kids don't need a perfect house. They need a house where they're expected.
- If your child has a drawer, a shelf, a hook for their backpack — you've already done more than you know.

Reflection Questions

- Does your child have their own defined space in your home — not just a bedroom, but items that belong specifically to them there?
- What is one consistent routine you currently have at your house?
- What is one you could add?
- If you're a long-distance dad, what could you do during the next visit to help your child feel less like a guest and more like a resident?
- What did home feel like to you as a child? What element of that can you re-create for your kid?

Every child who walks between two homes is carrying more than a backpack. They're carrying the ongoing work of belonging to two places at once — of being fully themselves in two different rooms, with two different sets of rules, two different versions of ordinary. That's not a small ask. Dad's job isn't to eliminate the weight of that — it's to make sure that when they set it down at his door, they feel like they've arrived somewhere that is genuinely, unambiguously theirs. Not a stop. Not a visit. Home. It's built slowly, in small gestures, through Saturday routines and labeled drawers and posters hung with care. Start wherever you are. Start today.

CHAPTER 2

The Big Feelings

"The most important thing you can do when your child is hurting is not fix it. It's stay."

There's a feeling kids carry into divorce that doesn't have a clean name — it's not quite sadness, not quite anger, not quite fear, though it borrows from all three. It's the feeling of a world that shifted under their feet, and the exhausting work of figuring out which way is up. Most kids don't have language for it. Some kids can't even locate it until it bursts out sideways in a moment no one saw coming.

The hardest thing I've had to learn as a dad — and I mean learned, because it didn't come naturally — is that my instinct when my kids are in pain is to fix something. Say the right thing. Redirect. Explain.

Offer an alternative. All of that instinct, applied to a child's big feelings, almost always makes things worse. This chapter is about what kids need instead. It's about learning to be the container, not the solution.

The children in this chapter — and throughout this book — are composite characters. Their feelings are real. Their names and stories are invented. For more on how and why these stories were created, see the Introduction.

• • •

Carter, age 10

I got in trouble a lot the year my parents split up. At school, at home, everywhere. My teacher called my mom twice about my behavior and my mom called my dad and my dad called me, and nobody seemed to understand that I wasn't trying to be bad. I was just — I felt like I was full of something and I kept spilling.

I didn't know it was sadness. I thought I was just mad.

Dad and I had this one fight where I threw my backpack across the living room because he said it was time to stop playing video games. I mean, I threw it hard. It hit the wall and left a mark. And for a second I thought Dad was going to yell, because that's the thing — I was sort of daring him to yell. Like I needed something to push against.

But he didn't yell.

He sat down on the floor. Right there, cross-legged on the living room floor. And he said, "Come here."

I didn't move. I was still shaking a little. He said it again, quieter:

"Come here, buddy." And I went and sat down across from him and he didn't say anything at all for what felt like a really long time. He just sat with me.

Then he said, "I know this year has been really hard. I know you're carrying a lot."

And I just started crying. I hadn't cried in months. I'd been mad instead of sad for months. But right then, with him just sitting there on the floor not yelling, I cried.

He said, "I've got you. You're okay."

I don't think he fixed anything that day. My parents still weren't together. My life still felt sideways. But something in me unclenched.

Like I'd been bracing for something and I could finally stop bracing.

I still don't know how to say what I needed. But I think it was just that. Him sitting down. Him staying.

• • •

Sofia, age 12

For a long time, I thought the divorce was my fault.

I know that sounds strange. I'm twelve — I know kids don't cause divorces. But knowing something and feeling something are different things. And what I felt, for a long time, was that if I had been easier, if I hadn't needed so much, if I hadn't been the reason they argued about school stuff or activities or who was picking me up — maybe things would have been different.

I never said this out loud. I didn't want to make it worse. I just carried it.

My dad told me early on that the divorce wasn't my fault. I remember he sat me down and said the words specifically: "This has nothing to do with you. You didn't cause this and you couldn't have fixed it." I heard him. But I didn't believe it yet.

The thing is, he said it once. And then he didn't say it again for a long time.

So the feeling stayed.

What I needed — and I didn't know how to ask for this — was for him to say it more than once. Not just the big official speech. I needed him to say it on random Tuesdays. To mention it when we were in the car and nothing else was happening. "You know this is still not your fault, right?" I needed it to become a regular thing, not a one-time announcement, because the doubt came back all the time, and I needed the reassurance to come back just as often.

Eventually he started doing that. I don't know if he figured it out on his own or if someone told him, but one afternoon while we were driving to my gymnastics class, he said it out of nowhere: "I was thinking about you today. Just want to make sure you know — none of this is on you. Not any of it." I looked out the window so he couldn't see my face.

It took a long time for the guilt to go away. But him saying it over and over was the only thing that helped it go.

• • •

Marcus, age 7

Sometimes I cry and I don't know why.

It happens at Dad's a lot. Not because of Dad — just because. I'll be watching TV or eating my macaroni and then all of a sudden I feel like crying and then I'm crying. Dad used to ask "what's wrong?" and I didn't know what to say because I didn't know. Nothing was wrong.

Everything was wrong. I couldn't explain it.

One time I was crying on the couch and he sat next to me and he didn't ask anything. He just put his arm around me. We stayed like that for a long time. He didn't try to figure it out. He didn't turn the TV off.

He just held me and waited.

After a while the crying stopped. Not because anything changed. Just because sometimes it does.

Then we kept watching TV like normal.

I think about that a lot. He didn't ask what was wrong. He just held me. That was enough. It was actually the right thing, even though he didn't say anything at all.

Sometimes I think dads think they have to fix it. But holding is good too.

• • •

Isabelle, age 15

I didn't cry. I just stopped talking about it.

I know some kids get angry or fall apart or act out after their parents split up. I went the other direction. I became very calm and very fine.

I went to school, I did my homework, I saw my friends, I came home, I went to bed. I was very organized about being fine.

My dad tried to talk to me a few times in the first few months. He'd ask how I was doing and I'd say "good" and he'd nod and that was that. I think I gave off this signal — and I meant to — that said: this topic is closed. After a while, he stopped asking.

I needed him to keep asking.

Not in a heavy way. Not sitting me down for a feelings conversation, because I would have completely shut down. But just checking in.

Casually. "Hey, how are you, really?" Or a text: Thinking of you.

How's it going? Something that said: I see you, and I'm not fooled, and I'm not going anywhere.

What I was doing — I understand it now — was testing him. Testing whether he'd stay interested in my interior life even when I pushed him away. The answer I kept getting was: eventually he'd stop. And I took that as confirmation that I'd been right to close the door.

It wasn't until a therapist helped me put language to what I was doing that I was able to tell my dad any of this. He felt terrible. He said he thought he was giving me space. And he was — but space and absence look a lot alike from the inside of a closed room.

If he'd kept asking — gently, without pressure, without needing me to answer — I think I would have opened the door a lot sooner.

Tomás, age 9 My dad was gone for a long time. He was in the Army and he was deployed twice. The second time, while he was gone, my parents decided to get divorced. So when he came back, he came back to a different life than the one he left.

I didn't know how to feel about him at first. I was glad he was home — obviously. But I was also kind of mad, and the mad didn't make sense to me because I knew he had to go, I understood that, but my chest was full of this complicated feeling when I looked at him. Like, where were you? And also, I missed you so much. And also, now everything is different and I don't know where to put any of this.

Dad didn't rush me. That was the main thing.

He came home and he was patient. He didn't try to jump straight back in like nothing had happened. He let me be weird around him for a while.

He'd come to things — my soccer games, picking me up from school — and he'd just be there, consistent and steady, and he didn't make me talk about the feelings. He let me have them.

There was one night when I finally said, "I was mad you were gone."

Not about the divorce specifically. Just — gone.

He said, "I know. You're allowed to be." He didn't explain it away or defend himself or get hurt. He just said I was allowed.

After that, we talked more. Not all at once, but slowly. And the complicated feeling in my chest started to loosen up, a little at a time. I think the loosening happened because he waited. He didn't need me to be ready before I was ready.

• • •

Kai, age 12

My little brother Mateo is six. When we switch houses — when Mom's car pulls up or Dad's car pulls up — Mateo cries. Every time. He grabs whoever he's leaving and he cries, and then he grabs whoever he's going to and he cries some more, and eventually he settles down, but for the first few minutes of every transition there's crying.

I stopped crying a long time ago. I'm twelve, and also, someone has to hold it together.

I started feeling like my job was to be calm so Mateo could be upset.

Like I had to use up all my calm for both of us. I'd hug him when he cried. I'd tell him it was okay. I'd distract him with games or shows.

I was doing the thing parents do, except I was twelve.

I didn't cry. I didn't have room for it.

Dad figured it out, I think, around Christmas. He pulled me aside one night — Mateo was asleep — and he said, "I've been watching you.

You've been holding a lot."

I shrugged. I said something like, "Someone has to."

And he said, "No. That's my job. Your only job is to be a kid."

I didn't know what to do with that. I kind of wanted to argue. But he kept going: "You're allowed to have feelings too, Kai. You're allowed to fall apart sometimes. I've got Mateo. I've got both of you. You don't have to carry this."

I didn't cry that night either. But I cried in the shower the next morning for about ten minutes, which I hadn't done in months.

It helped that someone told me I didn't have to be strong. That the permission came from my dad made it feel real.

Pull Quotes "I didn't know it was sadness. I thought I was just mad."* — Carter, 10 "I needed him to keep asking."* — Isabelle, 15 "He didn't ask what was wrong. He just held me. That was enough." — Marcus, 7

Dad Insight

I'll be honest with you: sitting with my kids' emotions without trying to fix them is still the hardest thing I do. I'm a problem-solver by nature and by profession — I spent years as an attorney, where the entire point is to analyze a situation and find a resolution. That skill is worse than useless when your seven-year-old is crying at the dinner table and can't tell you why. The instinct to diagnose, redirect, explain, or offer a better perspective is almost magnetic. Resisting it is work.

But the kids in this chapter are telling us something important: what they need most, in the middle of the storm, is not a solution. It's a witness.

Children experience a wide emotional vocabulary during divorce, and it's worth naming the full range: grief (yes, grief — the actual thing, not a softer version of it), guilt, anger, fear, confusion, loyalty conflict, shame, and relief, sometimes all at once. The guilt piece catches a lot of dads off guard. Kids absorb blame for things that had nothing to do with them. They run through the logic — the arguments were often about schedules, money, the kids themselves — and they land in the wrong place. Sofia's story said it clearly: knowing something in your head is not the same as feeling it in your body. She needed to hear "this is not your fault" not once, not twice, but over and over, until the feeling caught up to the fact. Say it on regular Tuesdays. Say it in the car. Say it in a text. Make it a practice, not a speech.

The "listening without fixing" framework sounds simple, but it has specific, learnable components. First: let them finish. Don't interrupt with reassurance before they're done expressing the feeling. Even well-intentioned reassurance — "But you're fine! You're so strong!" — tells a child that their feeling is an obstacle to get past rather than something worth sitting with. Second: reflect back.

"It sounds like you're really frustrated." "That sounds really lonely." You don't need to solve anything. Just prove that you heard.

Third: stay physically close. Marcus didn't need words. He needed his dad's arm around him. Touch communicates safety in ways that language can't always reach.

A note on the difference between validating feelings and excusing behavior: they are not the same thing. Carter threw his backpack.

That's not okay, and addressing it was appropriate — but his dad was smart enough to read the sequence correctly: connect first, correct later. When a child is flooded with emotion, they are not in a place to receive instruction. Be with them in the feeling first. When they're regulated, you can talk about the backpack.

What about when the anger is aimed at you? This happens. After a deployment, after a stretch of missed calls, after a broken promise — sometimes you're the target. The instinct is to defend yourself.

Don't. A child expressing anger at you is, among other things, doing you the significant honor of believing you can handle it. Don't prove them wrong. "You're allowed to be angry with me" is one of the most powerful things a dad can say.

For older kids who go quiet — the Isabelles of the world — the answer is not to push harder or schedule a feelings conversation. It's to keep a low, consistent, non-pressured presence. A casual check-in. A text. "Hey, thinking about you." Then let them come. The trap is interpreting their silence as resolution and stopping the check-ins.

Don't stop. The door may be closed, but your presence at the door is the whole message.

On siblings: if you have more than one child, pay attention to who's holding things together for the others. The oldest child, or the most emotionally regulated one, can end up functioning as a junior parent. If you see that happening, name it explicitly — like Kai's dad did — and redistribute the weight. Tell them specifically: your job is to be a kid. I've got the rest. Then prove it.

And finally: if you are seeing signs that your child's distress is not resolving — withdrawn for months, grades dropping, refusing to see friends, expressing hopelessness — please don't wait. A therapist who specializes in children and family transitions is not a crisis intervention; it's a resource. The distinction between normal grief and something that needs more support is sometimes clear and sometimes not, and a professional can help you read it. Seeking that help is not admitting failure. It's parenting.

Key Reminders

Your child's feelings are not problems to be solved. They are experiences to be witnessed.

Saying "this is not your fault" is not a one-time speech. It is a practice.

Silence is not peace. Keep asking, keep the door open, keep showing up.

Reflection Questions

Think about the last time your child expressed a big feeling — anger, tears, withdrawal. What was your first instinct? Did you fix, defend, or listen?

Have you told your child, in plain words, that the divorce is not their fault? Have you said it more than once?

What does your child look like when they're struggling but not saying so? What are the signals you may have learned to read?

Is there a feeling your child has expressed that you've found difficult to sit with? What would it look like to sit with it anyway?

At the end of this chapter, I want to leave you with one image: a child trying to hand you something heavy. They've been carrying it alone for a while. They're holding it out. Maybe with words. Maybe with tears.

Maybe with a slammed door or a silence that doesn't quite make sense.

What they're handing you is the thing they don't have the strength to hold alone anymore. Receiving that — without flinching, without redirecting, without rushing to set it down — is one of the most profound things a father can do. Not because it fixes anything. Because it says: I see what you're carrying, and I'm not going anywhere.

That's the whole message. That's everything.

CHAPTER 3

Holidays, Birthdays, and Traditions

"Traditions are not about the past. They are about who you are becoming together."

There's a particular silence in a house on Christmas morning when half the people who are supposed to be there aren't.

I know that silence. The first holiday season after a divorce has a texture that's hard to describe — it's not grief exactly, though it borrows from grief. It's more like standing in a familiar room where the furniture has been rearranged. Everything is technically fine.

Nothing is where it used to be.

Kids feel this acutely. Holidays and birthdays are the landmark moments of the family calendar — the days that were supposed to be fixed points, reliable and joyful. When divorce reshapes them, kids grieve the loss of what they expected those days to be. But this chapter isn't a chapter about loss. It's a chapter about what comes after. Because kids are not only capable of loving new traditions — they often come to love them fiercely, in ways that surprise everybody. If dad is willing to build something new.

The children in this chapter — and throughout this book — are composite characters. Their feelings are real. Their names and stories are invented. For more on how and why these stories were created, see the

Introduction.

• • •

Emma, age 8

The first Christmas at Dad's house, I woke up and I didn't know where I was for a second. Then I remembered. I was at Dad's. This was Christmas. This was the new Christmas.

It felt wrong at first. Not terrible, just off. Like a song played in the wrong key — you can tell it's the same song but something's different. I kept thinking about the old Christmas: waking up in my old room, the smell of Mom's cinnamon rolls, the pile under our old tree.

Dad's apartment tree was smaller. The ornaments were different — he'd bought a whole new set because the original ones stayed at the house.

I tried not to show how sad I was because Dad was working so hard. He had lights up and stockings on the mantle and he'd wrapped everything in the same paper and ribbons I usually liked. He was trying really hard.

Then he did a thing.

He made pancakes shaped like Christmas trees. I don't know how he did it — he must have practiced, because they were actually tree-shaped, with a little star at the top made of banana. He put green food dye in the batter. He let me add the chocolate chips for the ornaments.

It was so silly. It was so specific. It was entirely our thing.

That night, before I went to sleep, he asked me: "Do you want to do the pancakes again next year?" And I said yes immediately. And he said, "Good. It's ours now."

We do it every year. It's my favorite part of Christmas, which is strange to say, because the tree pancakes weren't part of Christmas before.

They're something we invented. But now they're real, and they're mine, and they belong to Christmas as much as anything else ever did.

Christmas is different now. But different and good can be the same thing.

• • •

Liam, age 11

My birthday is October 14th. Sometimes that falls on a week when I'm with my mom, which means I'm not with my dad on my actual birthday. The first year that happened, I was turning nine, and I thought it would be fine — Dad would just call and we'd do something the next time I was at his house.

It didn't feel fine. I mean, we talked on the phone and it was nice.

But it wasn't the same.

The next year, when it happened again, Dad texted me the morning of my birthday and said: "I'm going to need a full report on your birthday.

But also — I'm planning something. Be ready." He didn't tell me what.

When I got to his house that weekend, he had made it into its own thing.

He'd gotten a cake — not a store cake, a real one, from the bakery we like — and it said "Happy Birthday, Liam" in my favorite colors, blue and green. He'd wrapped presents. He'd made my favorite dinner: ribs and corn on the cob. He called it my "Dad Birthday."

The thing about the Dad Birthday is that it has no competition. My actual birthday has all this pressure — it's the real birthday, so it has to be the best, and usually there are other people around and it gets complicated. The Dad Birthday is just mine and his. Just us. He puts on whatever playlist I want, we eat ribs, and we don't have to share the day with anyone.

I look forward to the Dad Birthday more than my actual birthday. I'm not exaggerating. I've thought about this.

Don't tell my mom.

• • •

Zoe, age 14

The first few years of holidays after my parents split were kind of a disaster. Not screaming-fighting disaster, more like awkward-and-everyone-pretending disaster. Christmas at Dad's felt like we were doing a performance of Christmas. Easter at Mom's felt the same way. Like we all knew the script had changed but nobody was saying so.

I think what made it weird was that everyone was trying too hard to make it normal. And the trying was obvious. You can feel when adults are performing cheerfulness. It makes the cheerfulness feel fake, which makes everything feel worse than if no one had bothered.

Then the summer I was thirteen, my dad did something different. We were talking about the upcoming holidays and he said, out loud, "I know the holidays have been strange since we split up. I think it's been hard for all of us." He didn't say it sadly — just matter-of-factly, like he was describing the weather.

And then he said: "It's different now. But different doesn't mean bad."

I needed to hear that. Not in a therapy kind of way — just someone acknowledging what was real instead of pretending it was fine when it wasn't. Once he said it, I could relax. I didn't have to pretend anymore either.

After that, we kind of built our own holiday rhythm. Some things are still sad — like there are moments on Christmas Eve when I miss having everyone in the same house. I'm not going to pretend otherwise. But there are also things about my dad's Christmas that I love specifically because they're his. The way he does a movie marathon on Christmas Eve.

The fact that he lets me sleep in and we open gifts at noon. None of that would exist if everything had stayed the same.

I'm fourteen now. I'm old enough to know that grief and love can live in the same room. The holidays prove it every year.

• • •

Kenji, age 6

Daddy has a new family for Christmas now.

There's Laura, who is his new wife, and there's her kids — Marcus who is eight and Lily who is nine. So now when I go to Daddy's for Christmas, there's a lot more people. The first time, I felt kind of small. The tree was big and there were a lot of presents and Marcus and Lily already knew where everything was at Daddy's house and I didn't.

Lily and Marcus knew which drawer had the tape for the wrapping paper.

They knew which mug was the Christmas one with the peppermint. I didn't know those things.

I told Dad that I felt like a guest. He sat with me in the hallway and asked me what would help me feel less like a guest. I thought about it and I said: "If some of the ornaments were mine." On the old tree, before the new family, I had ornaments with my name on them. Baby Kenji and Kenji Age 3 and Kenji Age 5.

For that Christmas, they were still on the tree. But in all the moving around they had gotten mixed in with everyone else's. They weren't in a special place.

Dad went and found all my ornaments and moved them to the front of the tree, the part you see first when you walk in. My name, in the front.

It was a bigger table than before. It was louder and more crowded. But my ornaments were in the front, and everyone could see my name when they walked in.

I'm learning to like the bigger table. I'm not all the way there yet.

But I like that my name is on the tree.

• • •

Aaliyah, age 10

We celebrate Eid, not Christmas. My family is Muslim, and the big holidays for us are Eid al-Fitr at the end of Ramadan and Eid al-Adha later in the year. Before my parents split up, Eid was big — my grandparents and aunts and uncles would come, Mom would cook for two days, I'd get new clothes and gifts and we'd go to prayer at the big mosque and then eat for basically the whole day.

After the divorce, the first Eid was at Mom's. I wasn't with Dad during that one. The second Eid, I was supposed to be with him.

I was scared it wasn't going to happen. Dad isn't Muslim — my mom was — and I thought he might not know what to do, or he might forget, or he might treat it like a normal day. I didn't want to bring it up because I didn't want to make things awkward. So I just kind of waited.

The week before Eid, Dad texted me: "I've been reading about Eid. I want to do this right. Can you help me?"

I don't know how to explain how much that meant. He had researched it.

He was asking me.

We went to the smaller mosque near his apartment — the one I'd been to once before — for the Eid prayer. He wore the nice button-down shirt and he sat respectfully in the back while I prayed with the women's section. Afterward, we went to a halal restaurant he'd found, and he let me order everything I wanted. He got me the new outfit, which he'd asked my mom to help him pick out.

It wasn't the same as the big family Eid at Mom's house. I missed my grandparents and the noise and the two days of cooking. But Dad showed up for my religion when he didn't have to. He put in the work to understand something that wasn't familiar to him.

That's the thing that matters most. Not doing it perfectly. Trying.

Pull Quotes "He made pancakes shaped like trees. Now it's ours."* — Emma, 8 "The 'Dad Birthday' is actually my favorite one. Don't tell mom." — Liam, 11 "He said, 'It's different. But different doesn't mean bad.' I needed to hear that." — Zoe, 14

Dad Insight

The first Christmas after my divorce, I drove past a neighborhood full of lit-up houses and felt something I still don't have a clean word for. Not quite envy, not quite sadness — more like a specific awareness of absence. My kids weren't in the car with me. They were doing their Christmas. I was doing mine. And the two Christmases existed in parallel, in the same night, and that was going to be true from now on.

I did what a lot of dads do in that first year: I overcompensated. Too many presents. Too much decorating. Too much of everything. I was trying to make it so good that the fact that it was different wouldn't matter.

What I learned — slowly, over a few years — is that extravagance doesn't actually soften the grief. It just adds noise to it.

Here's what I want you to hear about holiday grief: it's the right word. When kids feel sad at Christmas or Thanksgiving or Eid or at their birthday, they are grieving a version of the day that no longer exists.

That's legitimate. Do not rush past it. Do not paper over it with activities or gifts or cheerfulness. Let it be there for a moment.

Zoe's story is clear on this: what helped was her dad naming the reality. "It's different now." Once that was said out loud, she could breathe. The performance stopped. And in that space, something real could grow.

The trap of overcompensating is worth lingering on because it's so common. Expensive experiences, piled-on gifts, relentless activity — these aren't bad things, but they can communicate to a child that the adult is uncomfortable with the grief and needs to cover it up. Kids read that. What they actually need is a dad who can sit with the complicated feeling alongside them and still bring something warm to the table.

So what makes a new tradition actually stick? A few principles: First, involve the kids in creating it. Don't just impose a new tradition — ask what they'd like, and build it together. Emma's Christmas-tree pancakes worked because she was a part of making them (adding the chocolate chips, choosing whether to repeat it next year). Second, keep it low-stakes. The best traditions are simple enough to sustain. The Lego-complexity version of a tradition collapses under its own weight.

Third, repeat it. Once isn't a tradition. Twice is starting something.

Ten times is something they'll describe to their own kids someday.

On birthdays specifically: the "Dad Birthday" is one of the most underutilized and effective tools in a divorced dad's kit. If you don't share the actual birthday, don't fight over it and don't make your child feel guilty for celebrating with the other parent. Create your own version — separate, uncompetitive, and fully theirs. The thing that makes it special is that it belongs to your relationship alone. No one is dividing it.

If a blended family is in your picture: holiday logistics become more complex, but the core principle doesn't change. Make sure your child's presence in the new configuration is visible. Their ornaments. Their traditions brought forward, not erased. Kenji needed his name on the front of the tree — not because he needed to win, but because he needed to know he wasn't disappearing. Think about where your child's name goes in the new picture. Then put it somewhere everyone can see.

For families with cultural or religious traditions — Eid, Hanukkah, Diwali, Lunar New Year — please hear this directly: it's your responsibility to carry those traditions forward, not defer them to your co-parent because they're "her side." If your children have a faith practice or a cultural heritage that you don't share, do the work. Read about it. Ask your child to teach you. Show up. Aaliyah will remember for the rest of her life that her father researched Eid and took her to prayer and found the halal restaurant. Not because he did it perfectly.

Because he tried.

Finally, on co-parenting around holidays: it's worth having a direct conversation — through a parenting app or email if face-to-face is difficult — about major holidays in advance. Not to fight over them, but to plan around them. The goal is not to "win" Christmas. The goal is for your child to experience Christmas, in whatever form, without absorbing your unresolved conflict about the schedule. That's a high bar. It's worth reaching for anyway.

Key Reminders

Kids don't need a perfect holiday. They need a present dad and a pancake that says you tried.

New traditions aren't replacements. They're additions. Give them time to become beloved.

Grief on a holiday is not failure. It's love. Make room for both.

Reflection Questions

What is one holiday or tradition that has felt awkward or painful since the divorce? What is one small thing you could do differently this year?

Does your child have something that belongs only to your time together on holidays — something that is uniquely yours?

If your family has cultural, religious, or ethnic traditions: are you carrying those forward on your end? If not, what would it take to start?

Have you ever asked your child what they wish your holidays together looked like? What might they say?

Children are the historians of family traditions — they remember everything. The ornament that goes in the front. The green pancake batter. The Dad Birthday cake with the blue and green frosting. The dad who showed up at the mosque in his good shirt. These are the stories they will carry for decades, and pass forward to their own children someday, usually with warmth and without the complications you're feeling right now. The new traditions a dad builds this year — small, imperfect, specific — will become the stories his kids tell. That's not pressure. That's an invitation. Start small. Start this year. Let it be yours.

CHAPTER 4

What Hurts

"Children are like wet cement. Whatever falls on them makes an impression." — Dr. Haim Ginott This is the hardest chapter in this book. I want you to know that before you read another word.

Every story that follows is real in the ways that matter — rooted in the emotions and experiences of children navigating divorce, drawn from the documented patterns therapists and researchers have observed for decades. These are composite voices. But the feelings? Those are exact.

What the kids in this chapter describe are not dramatic, cinematic traumas. They are the everyday accumulations — a dig here, a broken promise there, an exchange in a parking lot that felt like a weather system moving in. If you've been through a divorce, you've probably been part of at least one of these scenarios. Maybe more. Not because you're a bad dad. But because divorce is painful, and humans under pain behave in ways they wouldn't otherwise choose.

The goal of this chapter is not guilt. It is clarity. Discomfort, if it comes, is useful information.

The next chapter is about what helps.

The children in this chapter — and throughout this book — are composite characters. Their feelings are real. Their names and stories are invented. For more on how and why these stories were created, see the Introduction.

• • •

Alex, age 11

I know my parents don't want to talk to each other. I figured that out early. What I didn't figure out until later was that I was the one they had decided would talk for them.

It started small. Dad would ask me at pickup if Mom had said anything about the schedule for Thanksgiving. Or Mom would say, "Tell your dad the check is late." I'd carry it in my head the whole drive — rehearsing the words, worrying I'd get them wrong, worrying that however I said it would start something.

I got good at it. That was the problem. I got so good at carrying messages that they stopped realizing they were sending them. "Just ask your dad if he's okay dropping you off at seven." "Let your mom know I need the insurance card back." I had a whole separate brain for this — a filing cabinet just for their logistics.

My friend Marcus's parents would text each other sometimes. I remember thinking that was the most normal thing in the world and also something I had never seen. My parents communicated through me the way people used to send letters through someone on horseback. I was the horse. I was eleven.

The worst part wasn't the stress of it. The worst part was what it did to me inside. When I was at Mom's house, I felt like a spy for Dad — like everything I saw or heard was information he might want. When I was at Dad's, I felt the same thing in reverse. I couldn't just be in a place. I was always between two places, carrying things that weren't mine to carry.

I wasn't a kid anymore. I was a telephone.

I'm thirteen now. They still do it sometimes, without thinking. And I still carry it. But now I know what it is, and knowing doesn't make it lighter.

• • •

Lily, age 9

My dad doesn't yell about my mom. He's not that kind of dad. But he has a way of saying things.

Like when I came back from a week at Mom's and I was wearing new shoes and he said, "Huh. Guess she found money for that." He didn't say it loud. He said it quiet, to himself, but in a way that I was supposed to hear.

Or when Mom picked me up late one Tuesday and he said, "Classic," and shook his head. Just that one word. Classic. Like the way she works, as if she's a type and the type is bad.

He always seemed a little surprised when I didn't laugh along with it.

Like we were supposed to be on the same team. And I am on his team. I'm on both teams and I'm on neither team and sometimes that's so hard that I have to go sit in my room.

Here's the thing nobody told me: I look like my mom. I sound like my mom when I'm excited about something. I roll my eyes the same way she does. So when Dad says something small and sharp about her, it doesn't feel like he's talking about a person far away. It feels like he's talking about part of me.

I can't explain that to him. I'm nine. I don't have the words.

What I have is this feeling I get in my stomach when he starts — this bracing, like I'm about to get cold water on me. I hold very still. I laugh if I think I should laugh. I look at my shoes.

He thinks I don't notice. I notice everything.

I love my dad. That part I know for sure. But I also know that sometimes, in our house, loving him means pretending my mom is less than she is. And I'm not sure I can keep doing that without losing something.

• • •

Evan, age 13

The first time, I thought it was an accident.

Dad said he'd be at my basketball game — the Thursday one, the one that mattered because it was against Westside and I was starting for the first time. He wasn't there. He texted at halftime: Something came up, buddy. So sorry. Next one. I read it in the locker room and didn't cry because I was at school and you don't cry at school. I played the second half worse than the first.

Next one came. He wasn't there either.

By the fourth time — regional playoffs, my best game of the season, twelve points and three steals — I had already stopped looking for him in the bleachers when I walked out. I'd trained myself out of it. You can do that, it turns out. You can train yourself not to look.

My mom was always there. She worked the morning shift so she could make evening games. She sat in the same spot, third row, center. I looked for her without even realizing I was doing it.

For a while I kept telling Dad about the games. I thought maybe if I reminded him enough, if I made it easy enough, he'd show up. I texted him the times and the address. I drew him a map once, as a joke, to show him how close the school was. He laughed and said of course he'd be there. He wasn't.

After a while, I stopped inviting him. It was easier to not expect him.

I know he loves me. I know the games weren't the whole point. But here's what I learned from all of it: the way you find out how much you matter to someone is by watching what they do when it costs them something. My dad never seemed to calculate what his absence cost. I think he assumed I understood, assumed it was fine, assumed I'd get over it.

I did get over it. But I didn't forget. And now I'm thirteen, and I know something about my dad that I wish I didn't: he means what he says right when he says it. Just not long enough.

• • •

Camille, age 11

I used to get stomachaches on Fridays.

Not every Friday. Just the Fridays when Dad was picking me up. Which, for a while, was every other Friday, so — every other Friday, I had a stomachache.

It started around the time my parents stopped coming to the door for each other. Before, one of them would walk me up to the house and ring the bell, and whoever it was would say hi, maybe stand there for a second. That stopped. Now it was the parking lot of the apartment complex, or the driveway, and they would stay in their cars. I would get out and walk the space between them, dragging my bag, and feel the whole atmosphere of that space.

That's the only way I can say it: the atmosphere. You know how sometimes you can feel a storm before it actually starts? How the air changes? That's what the pickup felt like. Even when nothing happened — even when they both just nodded through their windshields and I walked the ten steps from one car to the other — I could feel everything they were not saying. The weight of it was enormous.

When there were words, it was worse. Nothing physical. Nothing loud, most of the time. But the tight voices, the clipped back-and-forth, Mom's hands getting still in a way that meant she was furious, Dad's jaw going hard. I learned every signal. I read them the way you'd read a forecast.

I would get in the car and Dad would ask how I was doing and I'd say "fine" and I meant something so far from fine that I couldn't have found a word for it in the dictionary. I meant: my stomach hurts and my hands are shaky and I'm so tired of being the person who walks between you and I just want to go home, and I don't even know which home I mean anymore.

The stomachaches stopped, eventually. I don't know exactly when. I think it was around the time my parents started being a little more — I don't want to say nice, that's not quite it — more quiet. Quieter.

Like they'd both agreed to let the storm be over.

I still notice the atmosphere. I think I always will. But at least now I can get out of the car without my hands shaking.

• • •

Noah, age 14

I'm going to try to say this fairly, because I think fairness is the only way it's honest.

Both my parents did it. Not just my mom, not just my dad. Both of them, at different times, in different ways, put me in the middle of something I didn't ask to be in the middle of.

With my mom it was the questions — casual ones, slipped in at dinner or on the drive home from school. What did Dad say about the vacation?

Does he seem happy? Is there a woman around? I answered them because she was my mom and I didn't know I could not answer. I didn't know I had a right to say I'm not doing this.

With my dad it was different. More direct, sometimes. He'd use the word unfair a lot, about the custody arrangement, about money, about the way things had gone. He wasn't entirely wrong — some of it was unfair. But I was thirteen and I didn't need to be his audience for it.

I didn't need to know the attorney's name or the specific numbers. I needed him to be my dad, not my confidant.

There were moments that were harder than I have words for. A moment, once, when I said something neutral — I don't even remember what — and my mom got very quiet and said, "So you're taking his side." And a moment, once, when my dad asked me directly: if I had to pick, if I had to choose, who would I choose? I was thirteen years old. He asked me that.

I didn't answer. I walked to my room and I closed the door and I put my headphones on and I thought about something I'd read in school about trees — how if you strip all the bark off one side, the tree will try to compensate, but it always leans. I felt like I understood that.

What I needed — what would have changed everything — was for one of them to decide to stop. Not for both of them to get along, not for everything to be fixed. Just for one parent to say: I'm opting out.

Not for my sake. For yours. One person to break the system.

Neither of them did it when I needed it most. I want to be fair about that, too.

I just needed one of them to stop. One.

• • •

Jade, age 11

I noticed the apartment was smaller before anyone said anything about it.

I noticed it at Dad's, I mean. We moved there six months after my parents split, and it was the two of us and this place that was maybe a third the size of our old house. Dad had set it up nicely — he'd gotten a new rug and hung up some pictures and there was a corner he made into mine, with a bean bag and my lamp from my old room. He was trying. I could see that.

But I noticed things. Like that we ate out less. Like that when I mentioned wanting a new pair of sneakers, his face did something quick and tight before he said "we'll see." Like that Christmas presents were fewer that year, and simpler, and he looked at me too hard when I opened them, like he was checking for disappointment on my face.

I learned to not ask for things. I learned it without anyone telling me to learn it. I just saw his face enough times and I understood.

The silence around money is its own kind of loud. Nobody sat me down and said, "Jade, things are tight." Nobody explained what had changed. But I felt it in every "we'll see" and every "maybe later" and every time he said "we don't need to go out tonight, let's cook something here" in a way that meant something different than "let's cook something here."

One night, a few weeks before my eleventh birthday, he sat down with me at the kitchen table and said, "I want to be honest with you about something." And for the first time, he explained it — not everything, not the numbers, not the attorney stuff. Just: the divorce cost both of us money, and things are different now, and that's real, and I know you've noticed, and I'm sorry I didn't say it sooner.

He was crying a little, which scared me. My dad does not cry.

But then he said something that I have thought about almost every day since: "We have less. But we have each other. And that part doesn't change."

I held onto that. I still do. Because I think I needed someone to say out loud what had been sitting in the air between us for a year. Love doesn't shrink when the house does. I know that now. But I needed him to say it.

• • •

Devon, age 10

I couldn't tell you when I stopped being able to pay attention at school. It happened slowly and then all at once.

My parents split up in October. By November I was sitting in class and my body was there but the rest of me was somewhere else entirely — running through logistics, mostly. Whose house tonight? Did Dad remember pickup at 3:15 or would I be standing by the fence waiting? If they both showed up, what would the parking lot feel like? What day was Wednesday?

I did that all day. I did it during math, which I used to be good at. I did it during reading. Mrs. Perez asked me a question once and I looked up at her and the answer was completely gone — not just the answer, but the question, the lesson, the whole room. She gave me this look, not mean, just worried, and I felt terrible about it.

My grades dropped. Three Bs turned into two Cs. My mom noticed and got scared and talked to my dad about it and they had a conversation that did not go well, because at that point most of their conversations did not go well. I heard some of it. It added to the logistics in my head.

Then one Wednesday, Mrs. Perez kept me after class. She said she'd noticed that I seemed far away this year, and she asked if everything was okay at home. I said yes, the automatic answer. She nodded. She didn't push.

But the next day, my dad called. He said Mrs. Perez had emailed him. He said: "I want to hear about what's going on in your head. What are you thinking about during school?"

And I told him. All of it — the logistics, the pickup questions, the Wednesday math class moment. He listened the whole time. Then he said:

"I'm going to call you on the nights I don't have you. Every night, before bed. Just to check in. So you know where things stand."

He did it. Every weeknight, even the ones I was at Mom's. Just a few minutes — how was school, is there anything for tomorrow, here's my plan for Wednesday pickup. It wasn't magic. But having the information meant I didn't have to run the calculations all day. I could just be in class.

My grades came back. Not all the way, not immediately. But they came back.

The point isn't that my dad fixed me. The point is that he saw what was actually happening, instead of just the symptom. He saw me. That was the whole thing.

Pull Quotes "I wasn't a kid anymore. I was a telephone."* — Alex, 11 "After a while, I stopped inviting him. It was easier to not expect him." — Evan, 13 "I just needed one of them to stop. One."* — Noah, 14 "Love doesn't shrink when the house does."* — Jade, 11

Dad Insight

When I was deep in my own divorce, I made some of the mistakes these kids describe. I won't tell you which ones — that's not the point — but I can tell you that I recognized myself in more than one of these stories. That recognition is its own kind of sting. It's not comfortable to see yourself in an eleven-year-old's account of what hurt her. But discomfort is honest, and honest is what this book is built on.

Here's what I want you to sit with before we talk about what to do: every single child in this chapter still loves their dad. Not one of them described a monster. They described a man under pressure, making choices that had costs — costs the kids absorbed quietly, often without saying a word. That's the thing about children and divorce: they're watching you far more carefully than you know, and they're far more forgiving than they probably should be.

The triangulation trap. Using your child to pass messages — even casual ones, even just once — places them in an impossible position.

They become responsible for managing the relationship between two people they love. Kids are not equipped for that, and it leaks into everything: their ability to relax at your house, their ability to relax at the other house, their ability to just be eleven. If you share a child with someone you can't talk to directly, use a co-parenting communication app — OurFamilyWizard, TalkingParents, AppClose. These tools exist precisely for this. The child should never be the channel.

Disparagement — including the quiet kind. The "huh" and the "classic" and the pointed silence. Kids hear all of it. And here is the part that matters most: your child is half of your ex. Their face, their laugh, their way of moving through the world — half of it came from the person you're making small. When you diminish your co-parent, even subtly, you are inviting your child to feel diminished too. This isn't about protecting your ex's feelings. It's about protecting your child's sense of identity and wholeness.

Broken promises are not minor disappointments. They are attachment ruptures. Every unkept promise is a data point, and children aggregate data. After enough data points, they stop hoping — not because they don't care, but because the pain of hoping became too expensive. The repair for this is not a speech. It is showing up, consistently, over time, until the data changes. If you've been part of this pattern, the only path forward is through.

The custody exchange. You control half of every pickup and drop-off.

That ten-second window in the driveway or the parking lot has its own emotional weather, and your child is reading every signal. The goal is not warmth toward your co-parent. The goal is neutrality — no tight jaw, no clipped tone, no loaded silences. Make the handoff boring. That boringness is safety.

Parental alienation — in yourself. I want to say this carefully, because it's easy to use this concept as a weapon in custody conflicts, and that's not what I'm doing. What I'm asking is this: look honestly at your own behavior. Have you asked your child to report on what goes on at the other house? Have you used the language of "choosing sides"?

Have you introduced the legal conflict into your child's awareness?

These behaviors — even when they feel justified — damage your child's relationship with themselves. And the research is unambiguous: kids who experience significant conflict between their parents have worse outcomes across almost every measured dimension. You cannot control the other house. You can control yours.

Financial stress and the silence around money. Kids absorb financial anxiety long before anyone explains it. They notice the smaller apartment, the quieter holidays, the "we'll see" face. Silence around these changes can feel like shame — like the family's reduced circumstances are something to hide, something to be embarrassed about.

The alternative is age-appropriate honesty: not the numbers, not the attorneys, not the blame — just the truth. Things are different now.

We have less in some ways. But here's what doesn't change. That sentence costs nothing and means everything.

Academic disruption as symptom. A child whose grades drop after a divorce is not struggling academically. They are struggling emotionally, and the struggle is showing up in the place where they're required to concentrate. The intervention is not tutoring — it's presence.

Calling on the nights you don't have them. Asking about specific assignments. Showing up in the logistics so they don't have to carry the logistics alone. Your engaged presence doesn't stop at the end of your custody week. It crosses that line. It has to.

And if you've been part of any of this — if you recognized yourself somewhere in these seven stories — here is what I want to say: don't use the recognition as an excuse to spiral into shame. Shame is not action. Awareness plus a decision to change, followed by consistent behavior over time — that's action. That's what these kids actually need.

Key Reminders

Your child is half you and half your ex. When you diminish one, you diminish the other.

A broken promise is not a small thing. To a child, it is a data point about their worth.

You cannot control what happens at the other house. You can only control what happens at yours.

Reflection Questions

Have you used your child to communicate with your co-parent — even casually, even once? What would a different approach look like, starting this week?

Have you made comments about your child's other parent in front of your child — directly or through implication? What impact might that have had on how your child sees themselves?

Think about promises you've made to your child in the last six months. How many did you keep? What pattern do you think your child has identified?

What would your custody exchanges look like if your only goal was to protect your child's nervous system? What would have to change?

Does your child know what is happening financially? Is there a version of the truth you could share that is honest without being burdensome?

The children in this chapter are not describing monsters. They are describing good people in hard situations making choices that had costs — and the costs were paid by kids who didn't have the vocabulary to name what was happening to them, only the body memory of stomachaches and trained-away hope and headphones and closed doors. The good news — the only news that matters at this point in the book — is that awareness changes behavior. Behavior, changed and held and repeated over time, changes outcomes. These stories are not indictments. They are invitations. The next chapter is about what helps. And what helps, it turns out, is often the precise mirror image of what hurts.

CHAPTER 5

What Helps

"Children need the freedom and time to play. Play is not a luxury.

Play is a necessity." — Kay Redfield Jamison If you asked your kid right now what helps the most — what actually makes the hardest days easier — what do you think they'd say?

Most dads guess wrong. They think about the vacation to Disney, the new game system, the big weekend. They think about gestures that cost something, efforts that announce themselves.

What the kids in this chapter describe is almost never that. It's the Tuesday night phone call. It's the dad who sat down next to his daughter and watched her show without asking what was wrong. It's the text that arrives every night like a heartbeat, so reliable that the one night it didn't come, she noticed immediately.

The good news is that none of this is expensive. The challenging news is that all of it requires consistency — which is harder than a single grand gesture, and worth so much more.

This chapter is a catalog of what actually lands.

The children in this chapter — and throughout this book — are composite characters. Their feelings are real. Their names and stories are invented. For more on how and why these stories were created, see the Introduction.

• • •

Nadia, age 9

Every night, my dad texts me before I go to sleep.

It says the same thing every time: "Good night, Nadia. I love you."

That's it. No emojis, no long messages, nothing extra. Just those two sentences.

I live with my mom most of the time. Three weeks out of four, roughly.

So a lot of nights I'm at her house, in my room with the purple curtains that I picked out when I was seven and still like even though I'm nine now, and at some point my phone lights up.

Good night, Nadia. I love you.

I started doing a thing where I look for it. Like before I even get tired, my brain has this little waiting thing going on — is it here yet? Most nights it comes right around 8:30. Sometimes closer to nine on weekends. Once, when he was at a work thing, it came at 10:47 and I had fallen asleep already but I saw it in the morning and it was still there.

The one time he forgot — this was maybe six months in, he was sick, some kind of fever thing — I didn't get it. I lay there waiting and it didn't come and I know this is going to sound babyish but I cried a little. Not loud crying. Just the kind that gets on your pillow.

He apologized the next morning. He said he had passed out early and he felt terrible. I said it was fine. But here is the thing about it not being fine: it wasn't fine because of how much the fine times mattered.

You only notice when something stops if it was really there to begin with.

That's how I know it's important. Not the night he forgot. Every single night before that.

He texts me every night. Even on mom's weeks. That was everything.

• • •

Tyler, age 12

My dad drove three hours round-trip to watch a soccer game that lasted sixty minutes.

It was a regular-season game. Not playoffs, not a tournament, not anything special. It was a Tuesday in March at the Greenfield Community Fields, field number three, which is the muddy one by the parking lot. I didn't even start — I came in for the second half.

He didn't tell me he was coming. I found out when I was subbing in and I looked over at the sideline and there he was, standing with his arms crossed, watching. He had a coffee cup. He was wearing the same jacket he always wears.

I didn't say anything to him about it until after. I just played.

After the game he came over and said, "Good second half, bud." That was it. He didn't make a big speech about driving three hours or about how much he loved me or about anything. He just said "good second half, bud" and messed up my hair and we walked to the parking lot together.

In the car — he drove me home, which added another forty minutes — I asked him why he came. He shrugged. "You had a game."

I thought about that for a long time after. You had a game. Like it was obvious. Like there was nothing else to say about it, no calculation, no sacrifice, no making-a-big-deal. You had a game, so I came.

My parents have been split up for two years. In those two years, I've learned to read people pretty well — I can tell when someone is doing something because they have to versus because they want to. My dad drove three hours for a muddy Tuesday game and didn't mention it again.

He didn't make a big deal about it. That was the point.

• • •

Grace, age 9

One afternoon in September I came home from school and I sat down at the kitchen table and I just felt really sad. Not about anything specific.

The kind of sad that doesn't have a name, that just sits on you like a heavy blanket.

My dad was in the kitchen making a snack. He looked at me and he didn't ask what was wrong. He made me a bowl of goldfish crackers — my favorite, the cheddar ones, not the pretzel kind — and he set it down in front of me and then he went and sat on the couch and turned on my show. My show at the time was this cartoon about a girl who can talk to animals. He just put it on.

I came and sat next to him. We watched. He didn't ask. I ate my crackers.

We watched three episodes. At some point I was leaning against him. By the third episode I felt better, and I still don't know exactly why.

Nothing had been said. The sad hadn't been explained or solved. He had just — been there. He'd noticed something was off and his answer to that was to make me my favorite snack and sit close.

I'm older now and I've had bigger things happen than that September afternoon. But I still think about it sometimes. I think about how sometimes the person you love doesn't ask what's wrong; they just move closer. That was what I needed that day more than anything. Not questions, not fixing. Just someone moving closer.

He just sat with me. We didn't talk. I still think about that day.

• • •

Mateo, age 8

My dad was sick for a while. The kind of sick where you have to go to the hospital a lot and then come home tired. My mom told me it was called chemotherapy, which sounds like science class, and that it was medicine that was hard on his body.

At the same time as the sick stuff, my parents were also splitting up. I didn't totally understand either thing, but I knew both were happening.

Dad couldn't come to some things he wanted to come to. He missed my birthday party — not the family dinner part, the school friend part with the jumping place. I knew he wanted to be there. He told me about thirty times that he wanted to be there. And he couldn't. He was too tired, and the doctor said no big crowds.

Here is what happened instead.

He called me from his couch, video call, and watched me open one present through the phone. Just one — he said pick the best one, so I picked the one from him. He watched my face when I opened it. He was wearing his favorite sweatshirt, the gray one, and he looked tired but happy.

He had sent a card to my teacher at school, asking her to tell me he was proud of me during the school day, which she did, and which embarrassed me but also felt good. He asked his friend Marcus — who is not my uncle but I call him Uncle Marcus — to come to my soccer game the Tuesday he couldn't make it. Uncle Marcus took pictures and sent them to Dad, and Dad texted me after: I watched you in those pictures. You looked great out there.

None of it was exactly right. None of it was him, in person, at the thing. But all of it was him. You could feel him in every piece of it.

He was trying, in every way the sick would let him, to be there.

I'm eight. I don't have a big word for what that taught me. I just know that showing up isn't only one thing. It's whatever you can manage when showing up costs you something.

• • •

Simone, age 16

I'm sixteen now. During the worst years — eleven, twelve, thirteen — my dad accepted less.

I mean that specifically. When my mom and my dad were figuring out the custody arrangement, things got hard, and instead of fighting for more time with me, he backed down. I think he was trying to keep the peace. I think he thought it was easier. I think maybe he believed that not pushing was a kind of love — not making waves, not causing more conflict, not making my mom angrier.

He was wrong.

Here's what I needed, that I didn't have words for at the time: I needed him to fight for me. Not for custody, exactly — not the legal thing. I needed him to communicate, through his actions, that being in my life was something he would not give up without a fight. What I got instead was a man stepping back politely. And when you're twelve and your parents are splitting up and you're trying to figure out your own worth in the world, a dad who steps back reads exactly one way.

It reads like you weren't worth the fight.

I know that's not what he meant. I know now, at sixteen, with more years between me and that scared twelve-year-old, that his backing down wasn't about me. It was about him — his own fear of conflict, his own grief. I understand it. I've forgiven it.

But I want to say it out loud, for whatever dad might be reading this:

When you accept less — fewer calls, fewer visits, less time, less involvement — because it's easier, because it avoids conflict, because you don't want to make things harder on everyone — your child is taking notes. And what they are writing down is this: I was not worth the difficult thing.

Fight for time with your kids. Not because of the legal arrangement.

Because of what it says. A dad who fights for presence is saying, every time, in every action: you are worth it. That message is everything.

That message is the one that lasts.

Pull Quotes "He texts me every night. Even on mom's weeks. That was everything."* — Nadia, 9 "He just sat with me. We didn't talk. I still think about that day." — Grace, 9 "I needed him to fight for me. A dad who fights for presence is saying: you are worth it."* — Simone, 16

Dad Insight

The chapter you just read is the reason I keep showing up on Saturday mornings with pancake batter and a messy kitchen. Not because pancakes are magic. Because consistency is. Because my kids learning that Saturday mornings are ours — predictably, reliably, boringly ours — is one of the most important things I can give them. I didn't figure that out immediately after my divorce. But I figured it out, and I want to save you some of the time it took me.

What these kids are describing — the nightly text, the muddy Tuesday game, the crackers and the couch — is the research, lived out. We know from decades of work on attachment and child development that small, consistent gestures outperform large, infrequent ones in almost every measurable outcome. The vacation to Disneyland fades. The Tuesday night call remains. Children measure love in repetition, and every repeated gesture says: you are stable in my life.

What "showing up" looks like when circumstances limit it. Mateo's story is one I want every dad who is working, traveling, sick, or dealing with limited custody to sit with. Showing up is not one thing.

It is whatever intentional effort looks like in your specific situation.

A video call with eye contact. A note slipped into their bag before school. Asking a trusted person to carry your presence when you can't be there in body. Kids are not evaluating your perfection — they are evaluating your effort. They can feel the difference between a dad who couldn't be there and a dad who wasn't trying to be there. Don't assume they can't. They absolutely can.

The danger of passivity. Simone's story is the hardest one in this chapter, and I want to be direct about it. When dads accept diminished roles — fewer calls, fewer visits, less involvement in school — out of conflict-avoidance or exhaustion or a sense that it's easier on everyone, they are sending a message. The message is not the one they intend. For a fuller framework on navigating co-parenting conflicts without retreating from your role, I'd point you back to The Present Dad (Book 1 in this series), particularly the chapter on showing up with steady love. The principle there applies here: your child needs you to hold your position, not because of legal rights, but because of what your presence communicates about their worth.

Phone calls, texts, and video calls as legitimate presence. There is a tendency among dads — particularly those dealing with distance, demanding work schedules, or limited custody — to feel that anything short of in-person contact "doesn't count." This is not what the kids say. What the kids say is that the text at 8:30, the call from the hotel room, the video chat where Dad showed up tired but showed up — these register. They accumulate. They become the heartbeat. If you can't be there in person, be there deliberately in every other form available to you. Presence is not always physical. But it is always intentional.

The secondary events. Tyler's dad drove three hours for a muddy Tuesday game on field number three. Not the tournament. Not the championship. The regular-season, Tuesday, nobody-watching game. There is something in this that goes beyond the act itself: it communicates that your child's ordinary life — not just their milestone moments — is worth your time. The school play where they have two lines. The science fair where they didn't win. The band concert where they're in the back row. These are the events where your presence says the most, precisely because the occasion doesn't seem to demand it.

Noticing as a skill. Grace's dad didn't ask what was wrong. He noticed something was off and moved closer. This is a learnable skill, and it's more valuable than most communication techniques. Pay attention to your child's emotional weather — not to fix it, not to diagnose it, but to register it. Then move closer. Sit down. Put on their show. Make the crackers. You don't have to have the right words.

You have to be in the right place.

Available versus present. These are not the same word. A dad who is physically in the house but on his phone is available. A dad who is sitting on the couch, show on, crackers on the table, is present. The distinction is not about devices or screen time. It's about attention.

Your child can feel the difference between your body being in the room and your attention being in the room. They want the second thing. They will take the first one if that's what they can get, but they notice the gap.

Key Reminders

It doesn't have to be big. It has to be consistent.

Showing up when it's inconvenient tells your child exactly where they rank.

Presence is not always physical. But it is always intentional.

Reflection Questions

What is one small, consistent thing you currently do that your child might quietly depend on? Are you protecting it?

- Think of the last time you "showed up" in an inconvenient or unexpected way. What did your child's reaction tell you?
- Are there ways you've accepted a diminished role — fewer calls, fewer visits, less involvement in school — out of conflict-avoidance? What would reclaiming that role look like?
- What is one thing you could start doing this week — small, consistent, low-effort — that your child would notice within a month?

Come back, for a moment, to the Tuesday night phone call. Not the vacation. Not the birthday party. Not the gesture that required planning and money and a cleared calendar. The Tuesday night call — the one that costs nothing except the intention to make it, the one that has happened so many times it has become part of the architecture of your child's week. That call is the whole argument. That call is what children mean when they say, years later, that their dad was there for them — not because they remember the content of any specific conversation, but because the call kept coming, reliable as weather, dependable as morning. Every time a dad shows up — especially when it's inconvenient, especially when he's tired, especially when it would be so easy to let it go just this once — he is answering a question his child is always, quietly asking. The answer is the same every time: Yes. I'm still here. You can count on me.

CHAPTER 6

Looking Ahead

"Children are not a distraction from more important work. They are the most important work." — C.S. Lewis Children of divorce are future-oriented in a specific, anxious way. They spend real mental energy trying to calculate what comes next. Will Dad start dating? Will he remarry? If he gets a new family, will there still be room for me? Who walks me down the aisle? Will they fight at my graduation?

These are not irrational questions. They're not manipulation, either.

They are the natural projections of a child who has already learned — the hard way — that family structures can change without warning. A child who once believed the future was stable and found out it wasn't doesn't stop imagining the future. They just start imagining it with more fear.

This chapter holds those questions with respect. And it asks dads to do the same.

The children in this chapter — and throughout this book — are composite characters. Their feelings are real. Their names and stories are invented. For more on how and why these stories were created, see the Introduction.

• • •

Mia, age 13

I found out my dad was dating because I saw a text on his phone. I wasn't snooping — it was just sitting there face up on the counter while I was getting a glass of water, and her name came up with a little heart emoji next to it. That was six months ago, and I still think about that moment more than I probably should.

I want my dad to be happy. I really do. When he's lonely I can feel it, the way the apartment gets this certain kind of quiet that's different from regular quiet. He watches TV with the volume too loud and eats dinner standing up at the counter instead of at the table. I don't like seeing him like that.

But the heart emoji kind of knocked the wind out of me.

I didn't say anything. I just took my water and went back to my room and lay on my bed and stared at the ceiling. I kept thinking: what if she's there when I come over? What if she has kids? What if he likes being with her more than he likes being with me? That last one is the one I'm most ashamed of, because it sounds selfish, but it's also the truest one.

He brought it up himself about two weeks later. We were driving to get tacos — just us, a Friday night thing we do — and he turned down the radio and said, "Mia, I want to talk to you about something." And I already knew what it was, and my stomach dropped, and I thought: here we go.

But then he said something I didn't expect. He said, "I'm not going to introduce you to anyone until you're ready. And I'm not going to pressure you to be ready. I just wanted you to know that you come first.

You always come first. Okay?"

I looked out the window so he wouldn't see me cry.

He didn't rush it. He checked in with me every few weeks — not in a big dramatic way, just casually, like, "You still feel okay about things?" The actual introduction, when it finally happened, was low-key. A coffee shop. An hour. She was nice. I'm not sure how I feel about all of it yet. But I know my dad handled it the right way, because the whole time, I felt like he was watching out for me. That made the hard parts easier to get through.

• • •

Ben, age 16

I started dreading graduation about eight months before it happened.

Not because I wasn't excited — I was, genuinely. But every time I imagined the day, I saw the seating chart problem: where does Mom sit, where does Dad sit, how do we do pictures, what happens if they have to stand next to each other, what happens if one of them says something to the other one and it turns into a thing? My graduation becoming a "thing" was my biggest fear.

I'd watched it happen at my cousin's graduation two years earlier. Her parents had a whole scene in the parking lot. She cried in the bathroom during the reception. I swore that wasn't going to be me.

My dad picked up on it before I even said anything. He asked me one night what I was looking forward to about the end of the year, and I gave him this kind of vague answer, and he sat with it for a second and then said, "Are you worried about graduation? About how the day's going to go?"

I said yes. I said I was kind of scared it was going to be ruined.

He didn't get defensive. He didn't say, "Your mom and I are adults, Ben, we can handle it." He just nodded and said, "That day is yours.

You hear me? That day belongs to you. And I will do whatever I need to do to make sure you feel that."

He called my mom the next week — I found out later — and they actually talked about a plan. Who sat where. The pictures logistics. A time buffer so they weren't arriving at the same time. Nothing elaborate. Just thoughtful.

Graduation day, I walked out in my cap and gown and both my parents were sitting on opposite sides of the gymnasium and both of them were crying and I thought: this is mine. This is actually mine.

I didn't cry until I got home.

• • •

Ava, age 10

I asked my dad once if he was going to get a new family.

I know that sounds like a weird thing to ask. But we were watching a movie where a dad got remarried and had new kids, and I kept looking at the kids in the movie and wondering if they felt what I was feeling, which was: where do I fit now?

My dad turned off the movie and sat with me on the couch and asked me what was going on. I told him I was worried that if he got new kids, I wouldn't be his favorite anymore. I felt embarrassed saying it, but he didn't make it weird.

He said, "Ava. You are my daughter. That is not a job I'm going to give to someone else." And I said, "But what if you have more kids?"

And he said, "Then they'd be your siblings, and you'd still be my Ava. Nothing changes that."

I needed him to say it exactly like that. Not "of course" or "don't be silly." I needed the specific words.

He still says it, actually. Not every day — that would be weird — but he works it in. When he drops me off at school sometimes he'll say, "Have a great day, my girl." My girl. That's what I hold on to. Not just that he said it once, but that he keeps saying it.

Sometimes I still get scared that things are going to change in ways I can't predict. But then I remember that he's told me. Repeatedly. And I think maybe the knowing isn't something you just collect once — maybe it's something dads have to keep giving, and kids have to keep hearing, until it finally settles somewhere deep enough to stay.

• • •

Jordan, age 17

Everybody keeps asking me if I'm excited about college. And I am. But there's this thing I haven't told anybody, because it sounds strange.

I'm scared of what happens to my relationship with my dad once the custody schedule ends.

Right now I see him every other week. There's a calendar, a plan, a routine. I know when I'm going to his house and he knows when I'm coming. That structure has been my whole life since the divorce. And in three months I'll be at a school five hundred miles away and there won't be a calendar anymore. Just — what? A text when I feel like it?

A phone call on holidays?

I love my dad. I know he loves me. But I've watched other kids whose parents divorced go off to college and just... drift. Dad stops calling as much because he figures you're busy. You stop going home as much because it feels complicated. And then you look up at twenty-five and realize you don't actually know each other anymore.

That was the thing keeping me up at night.

My dad must have figured something out, because about six weeks ago — I hadn't said any of this to him — he sat me down and said he wanted to talk about what our relationship was going to look like after I left.

He said, "I want to make sure you know that my involvement in your life doesn't depend on a custody schedule. I'm your dad regardless. I want to build that with you now, before you go."

We decided on a weekly Sunday call. Not mandatory, but intentional. He said he'd always answer, no matter what.

I can't explain exactly why that helped so much. It's just a phone call. But somehow knowing it was coming — that he'd thought about it, that he'd set it up without me having to ask — was the thing I needed. It told me that the calendar wasn't why he showed up. He shows up because I'm his kid.

I think I can go now.

• • •

Diego, age 8

My dad has a girlfriend named Renee. She has two kids, Tyler and Amara.

Tyler is nine and Amara is six.

At first I didn't like going over when they were there. It's not that they were mean — they weren't. It's more like... I didn't know where to stand. My dad's apartment used to feel like mine. I had my corner of the couch. My cereal in the cabinet. My Legos on the shelf in the spare room. And then suddenly there were other kids there and Tyler sat in my corner and I didn't say anything but I felt it, the way you feel something when it's wrong even if you can't explain it.

I told my dad I didn't want to go over when they were there. He didn't argue. He asked me why, and I tried to explain the corner-of-the-couch thing, and he listened like that was a real thing and not a dumb thing.

He said, "Diego. I want to tell you something about how love works.

It's not like a pizza where you have to share the slices. The more people you love, the more love you have. Loving Tyler and Amara doesn't take anything from what I have for you."

I thought about that for a while. I wasn't totally sure I believed it yet, but I thought about it.

What helped more than the words was what he started doing. Every time we went over there together, he'd find at least one block of time —

even just an hour — that was just us. We'd take a walk, or shoot baskets, or sit in the kitchen and eat cereal together while Renee took the other kids somewhere. Just me and my dad. My corner.

He never stopped carving that out. And I started to believe the pizza thing a little more every time he did.

Pull Quotes "He said, 'That day is yours.' I didn't cry until I got home." — Ben, 16 "I needed him to say it exactly like that. Not 'of course' or 'don't be silly.' I needed the specific words." — Ava, 10 "Once the schedule ends, what's left? That was the thing keeping me up at night."* — Jordan, 17

Dad Insight: The Future Your Kids Are Already Living In

I think about the future more than I let on. Specifically, I think about what my kids' lives will look like in ten, fifteen, twenty years — and whether I'll still be in them the way I want to be. My daughter is nine and my son is ten right now, and the time I have with them at this exact age, at this exact level of need, is already slipping past faster than I know what to do with. I understand, from a place that is entirely personal, why these kids in this chapter are scanning the horizon the way they are. Because I'm doing it too.

What I've learned — and what the research consistently backs up — is that children's future-focused anxiety after divorce isn't irrational. It's protective. They've already seen the rug pulled out once, so they're running scenarios, trying to anticipate the next pull.

When a dad understands that, he stops hearing his kid's questions as manipulation or insecurity and starts hearing them as information: tell me I'm still safe. Tell me you're still mine.

If you're navigating a new relationship — dating, getting serious, thinking about introductions — slow down. Your child isn't asking you to stay alone forever. They're asking you to be deliberate. Mia's dad didn't delay the introduction to be dramatic; he delayed it because he paid attention to his daughter's emotional readiness and moved at her pace. The difference between an introduction that fractures trust and one that builds it is almost always timing and communication. For a full treatment of this — the when, the how, the what-not-to-do — read The Dating Dad (Book 4 in The Present Dad Series). I go deep on all of it there.

Milestones deserve a plan. Graduation, championships, performances, weddings — these are the days your child has been quietly pre-dreading. They shouldn't have to spend those days managing you and the other parent. Ben's dad understood something important: that reassurance without action is hollow. He said "that day is yours," and then he made it so, by calling the other parent and working out the logistics. That's what backing up a promise looks like.

The custody-schedule cliff is real, and most dads don't see it coming.

When the legal structure ends — when your teenager goes off to college or ages out of the order — the relationship doesn't automatically continue on its own momentum. You have to build the bridge before you get to the edge. Jordan's dad didn't wait to be asked. He initiated the conversation, named the transition, and set up a structure that said: I'm not here because the court said so. I'm here because you're mine. That is the conversation every dad of an older teenager needs to have before the calendar runs out.

Explicit reassurance is not optional. Ava's story is a reminder that children don't infer safety — they need it spoken. "Of course" isn't enough. "My girl" is. Find the specific words that match your child and use them on repeat. Not just once. Not just in the big moments. In the Tuesday-morning drop-off moments. In the text that says nothing except "thinking about you." The repetition is the message.

Finally: love is not a finite resource. If you're building a blended family, that truth will be tested constantly. Diego needed to hear it from his dad — but he needed to see it more. The words gave him a framework. The weekly one-on-one time gave him evidence. Both matter.

Start with the words, then put in the hours that make the words true.

Your child is already writing the future in their head. The question is whether they're writing you in it. You get a say in that. Use it.

Key Reminders

- Your child is already writing the future in their head. Make sure they know you're in it.
- Milestones belong to your child first. Plan accordingly.
- The custody schedule ends. Your fatherhood doesn't.

Reflection Questions

- Have you had an explicit conversation with your child about your role after the custody schedule ends — or about your long-term vision for your relationship?
- If you are dating or in a new relationship: how has your child been included in that transition? What signals have you sent, intentionally or not?
- What milestone is coming up in the next one to two years that your child might already be anxious about? What could you say or do now to address that?
- Imagine your child at thirty, describing your relationship. What would you want them to say? What would have to be true for that to happen?

The future that kids fear is a future where they are alone in it. Not unloved in a grand, abstract sense — most of them know, at some level, that their dad loves them. What they fear is something more specific: that the love will get reorganized, distributed to new people, swallowed up by new routines, and that by the time everything settles, there won't be a guaranteed place left for them. What they hope for — what every voice in this chapter is reaching toward — is a dad who is already in the picture they're drawing. Not perfectly. Not without complexity. But there. Present in the ordinary weeks and the milestone days and the phone calls that happen for no reason except that they're his kid and it's Sunday. That future is not determined by the divorce.

It is determined, slowly and daily, by what a dad does with the years that follow it.

CHAPTER 7

Love and Limits

"Children need love, especially when they do not deserve it."* — Harold Hulbert Divorced dads fall into one of two traps, and usually the trap finds them before they even realize they've stepped in it.

The first trap is the fun dad: the one who lets everything slide, avoids conflict at all costs, says yes to everything because he can't stand the thought of spending his limited time in friction. No bedtime. No homework rules. No consequences. Just — please, let this be a good weekend. Let me be the one they want to come back to.

The second trap is the overcorrector: the dad who read something about structure or heard something in a podcast and swung hard toward rigid enforcement, became harsh, barked orders at kids who were already confused and grieving, and called it fatherhood.

Both of these traps come from the same root: a dad who isn't sure where he stands with his kids and is trying, clumsily, to earn his place back.

The irony is that neither approach gives children what they actually need. And the kids in this chapter — in their own words, from their own experience — are here to tell you what that is.

The children in this chapter — and throughout this book — are composite characters. Their feelings are real. Their names and stories are invented. For more on how and why these stories were created, see the Introduction.

• • •

Oliver, age 11

When my parents first split up, my dad felt so bad about everything that he just kind of stopped saying no to me.

I mean that literally. No bedtime. I could stay up as late as I wanted.

Junk food whenever I asked. We never did homework at his house — he'd say, "You can catch up Monday." He let me skip a shower twice in a row once and didn't say anything. I got to play video games for basically the entire weekend, every weekend.

For about two weeks, I thought it was amazing.

Then it started to feel weird. Like — I'd ask for something, and he'd say yes, and instead of feeling good about it, I'd feel this hollow thing. Like the yes didn't mean anything anymore because it was always yes. I started asking for things I didn't even really want, just to see if he'd finally push back. He didn't.

Here's the thing I didn't know how to say then, but I do now: it felt like he didn't care. Not in a mean way. But when my dad stopped telling me to go to bed, it felt like he'd stopped paying attention to whether I was okay. When he stopped making me do my homework, it felt like he'd stopped caring about who I was going to become. When everything was yes, yes, yes, it was like he'd given up on — I don't know — the job of being my dad.

I missed the no. I know that sounds strange. But the no meant he was watching. The no meant I mattered enough to push back on.

We eventually talked about it — my mom actually brought it up with him — and things shifted. He started enforcing the bedtime again. Made me do homework after dinner before screens. It wasn't fun, exactly. But it felt safer. Like someone was in charge. Like someone was thinking about tomorrow, not just surviving this weekend.

• • •

Layla, age 12

For the first year after my parents separated, my two houses had completely different rules.

At Mom's: bedtime at nine, no phones in the bedroom, homework before anything else, no screens on school nights. At Dad's: no real bedtime, phone charging next to my bed, homework when I felt like it, TV whenever. I'm not blaming my dad — I think he just didn't know how to parent alone yet, and it was easier to let things go.

But I became a different kid depending on which house I was in. At Mom's I was organized and on top of things. At Dad's I was kind of a mess. My grades at school started to slip because my school week started on Monday and I was coming off Dad's weekend with no sleep and overdue assignments. I was tired and scattered and I didn't connect those two things at first.

Then my parents actually sat down — I think they went to a co-parenting counselor — and came up with an agreement about the basics. Not everything had to be identical. But the core stuff: bedtime, homework, screen time. They aligned on those.

The change was noticeable almost immediately. Not because the rules were so different, but because now both houses felt like they were pulling in the same direction. Like my parents, even though they didn't live together anymore, were still on the same team about me. Still coordinating. Still parenting me together even when they were apart.

That sounds like a small thing. It wasn't. It made me feel less split down the middle. It made me feel like one kid again, living in two places — instead of two different kids who happened to share the same face.

• • •

Jackson, age 9

My dad read a book about parenting. I know because he told me about it.

He said he'd learned that kids need more structure, and I didn't totally understand what that meant until the next weekend, when everything changed all at once.

Before the book, Dad was pretty relaxed. After the book, it was like the rules had all been rewritten in a new language and nobody told me.

Bedtime was now eight-thirty sharp. Homework first — no exceptions.

Screen time was limited to one hour. If I argued, he'd get loud and say something like, "Jackson, I'm trying to raise you right."

Here's what I want to tell him, that I didn't know how to say: I wasn't looking for a drill sergeant. I was looking for my dad.

The strictness didn't feel like love. It felt like he was doing everything by a checklist — like he was trying to be a good dad in a way he'd read about somewhere, instead of just being my dad. When he got loud at me for taking too long on homework, I didn't think, "Dad really cares about my education." I thought, "Dad's mad again." When he enforced the screen time with this tight-jaw expression, I didn't feel safer. I felt further away.

What I needed — what I think most kids need — is something in between. Rules, yes. Consistency, yes. But delivered with the same warmth that makes me want to follow them in the first place. A dad who looks me in the eye after setting a limit and says, "I love you, bud" before I go to bed. Not a speech. Not a stern face. Just the rule, and then the love, in the same sentence if possible.

The best nights at Dad's house are when he tells me to put the game away and I groan, and he kind of half-smiles and says, "I know. Bedtime anyway," and then tucks me in and talks to me for five minutes about whatever. That's it. That's what I'm looking for.

• • •

Ananya, age 14

I need to be honest about something: I was not a good kid the first year after my parents divorced.

I snuck out twice. I lied about where I was on three separate weekends.

My grades went from mostly A's to a C average in one semester. I stopped doing things I had always done — swim practice, tutoring a younger kid in my neighborhood I'd been doing since sixth grade. I just stopped.

My mom was scared. My dad, I think, was also scared, but he handled it differently.

He sat me down. Not a lecture — he literally just sat across from me at the kitchen table and said, "Ananya. Something's wrong. Tell me what it is." I said nothing was wrong. He said, "Okay. I'm going to be here anyway." And then we just sat there, which was uncomfortable, and eventually I started talking.

He didn't let me off the hook when I was clearly not behaving. He took my phone away for two weeks when I snuck out. He made me call the family of the kid I was tutoring and explain why I'd stopped. He drove me back to swim practice and sat in the bleachers while I got back in the pool.

He wasn't cruel about any of it — he didn't yell, didn't bring it up over and over. But he held the line.

I remember being so angry at him. Like: Dad, I am literally falling apart, and you're taking my phone?

But here's what I understand now that I didn't then: I was testing whether there was a wall. I'd already learned that the structures of my life could disappear — the marriage, the house, the routines. I needed to find out if my dad was going to disappear too, or if he'd stay solid. If he'd hold me even when I was being impossible to hold.

He held me. He was firm and he was present and he never withdrew the love even when he withdrew the privileges. That combination — that exact combination — was what stabilized me.

I needed to find the wall. I needed to know it was there.

• • •

Lucas, age 7

I know exactly what happens after dinner at my dad's house.

We put the dishes in the sink together. Then it's bath time — I get to choose the bath fizzy if I didn't argue too much about vegetables at dinner. Then Dad comes in and helps me with pajamas if I need it, or watches me do it myself if I don't. Then we go to my room and I pick two books. He reads them both. Even the long ones. Even when he's tired. Then lights out, and he sits on the edge of the bed and we talk about three things from my day. Best part, worst part, something I'm looking forward to tomorrow.

Then he says "I love you, bud," and I say "I love you too, Dad," and he turns on my star light and closes the door most of the way, not all the way.

I know all of that is going to happen. Every time.

Some of my friends have dads who don't always put them to bed. Or sometimes there's no routine and they just fall asleep wherever and then get moved. I feel kind of bad for them when they tell me that, even though I don't totally understand why yet.

What I know is this: when I'm at Dad's house, I never have to wonder what's coming next. And the not-wondering feels so good that sometimes, when I'm lying in the dark listening to Dad's footsteps after he closes the door, I feel this big warm safe feeling in my whole chest.

I think that feeling is what safe feels like. I'm pretty sure I'd miss it if it went away.

Pull Quotes "When everything was yes, it felt like he'd given up on the job of being my dad."* — Oliver, 11 "I needed to find the wall. I needed to know it was there."* — Ananya, 14 "I know exactly what happens after dinner. That not-wondering feels so good."* — Lucas, 7

Dad Insight: The Discipline of Love

Let me be honest about something before I give you any advice about discipline: I fell into the fun-dad trap myself. Not for long, but long enough to feel the quiet unease of a child who has been given everything and is somehow still searching for something. My kids would ask for another hour of screen time, and I'd say yes. Ask for junk food I normally wouldn't allow, and I'd say yes. And then I'd watch them go back to their phones, and I'd feel relieved that there was no conflict — and also feel like I'd let them down in some way I couldn't quite name. The instinct to be the "good" parent, especially when your time is limited and your guilt is running high, is powerful. But it's worth resisting.

The "fun dad" trap is almost always guilt-driven, and it almost always backfires in the same way: the child experiences permissiveness not as freedom, but as absence. When you stop saying no, you stop communicating that you're paying attention. You stop sending the signal that says I'm tracking you, I care about where you're going, I have an opinion about who you're becoming. Children need that signal. Even when they fight it. Even when they tell you they hate the rules. The fighting is normal. The need underneath it is not going away.

Authoritative parenting — warm, consistent, firm but not harsh — is what the research points to across every demographic, and the post-divorce context doesn't change that conclusion. It actually amplifies the need for it. Children navigating two homes, two routines, the emotional aftermath of a family rupture — they need to know that at least one of their environments is solid and predictable. If yours isn't, you're adding chaos to a life that already has plenty.

Here's the nuance, though — and Jackson's story makes this clear — strictness is not the goal. Consistency delivered without warmth just makes kids feel controlled. What you're after is something like this: you hold the limit, and you hold the relationship at the same time. You say no, and then you say "I love you, bud," and the two things are not in conflict. Accountability without love feels like punishment.

Accountability inside of love feels like security. The delivery matters as much as the standard.

On consistency across two homes: you don't have to be identical with your co-parent. You won't be, and the expectation that you can be is a setup for conflict. But on the fundamentals — sleep, school, safety — it's worth making the effort. Not for your sake or your co-parent's sake, but because your child is building their weeks, their sleep habits, their ability to function at school, out of whatever structure you collectively provide. Layla's story is a quiet argument for doing the hard work of co-parenting communication, even when that communication is uncomfortable.

For dads with limited custody time: the "I only have them three days, I don't want to spend it fighting" logic is understandable. But consider what three days of unchecked permissiveness actually costs your child — and your relationship. A kid who comes home from your house overtired, overfed on junk, and behind on homework is a kid who is learning that your house is where regulation breaks down. That is not the impression you want. You can have fun AND have structure. Saturday pancakes and an enforced bedtime are not opposites.

Finally, on repair: you will lose your temper. You will go too far or swing too hard or be inconsistent in ways that confuse your kids. When that happens, go back. Say the words. "I got angry and I shouldn't have said it that way. I love you. I'm still your dad and I'm still here." A repaired rupture often builds more trust than an unbroken one.

The repair shows them you're self-aware. That you're paying attention.

That the relationship matters enough to go back and tend to it.

A dad who holds the line — calmly, consistently, lovingly — is telling his child something they desperately need to hear. He's saying:

I am paying attention to you. I care about who you are becoming. And I intend to be around long enough to find out.

Key Reminders

Rules are not the opposite of fun. They are the architecture that makes fun feel safe.

A dad who holds the line — calmly, consistently, lovingly — is telling his child: I am paying attention to you.

Your child doesn't need you to be their best friend. They need you to be their father. Those are not the same thing.

Reflection Questions

Would your child describe your household as having clear, consistent rules? Would you? Is there a gap between those two answers?

Have you avoided enforcing a rule or consequence because it felt like it would damage the relationship? What did that teach your child?

Think about a recent conflict over discipline with your child. How was it resolved? What would you do differently?

If your child is acting out: is there any possibility they are testing whether you'll hold the line? What would it look like to hold it with warmth?

Here is the central paradox of this chapter: the dad who says yes to everything — who removes every limit, softens every boundary, gives every inch — is, from his child's point of view, a dad who isn't quite sure they're worth the effort of a no. Children know this, even when they can't say it. They experience the absence of limits as a kind of inattention. And what they want, underneath every test and tantrum and sullen teenage door-slam, is a father who is so certain of his love that he's willing to be the bad guy for it. Limits are not the opposite of love. They are one of love's most specific expressions — proof that a dad is watching, that he cares about who his child is becoming, and that he intends to be around long enough to find out. These kids are going to be okay. Not because the divorce didn't cost them something real. But because someone held the line. Go home and be that someone.

There's still time.

Back Matter

Afterword: A Letter to Your Child

Something happened to me in the writing of this book.

I had expected it to be clarifying — a way to organize and present what research and experience had taught me about children and divorce and the irreplaceable role of a present father. I thought I was building an argument. What I didn't expect was to feel, page by page, like I was sitting in the room with my own kids while they talked. Not because any of these composite voices belong to them — they don't. But because every emotion in every story is real. Because the longing underneath all these voices — to be seen, to be safe, to know their dad is still their dad — is the same longing I see when I look at my kids.

If these pages moved you, I want you to do something with that. Not just reflect on it. Not just bookmark it and return to it someday. Do something now, this week, before the feeling fades.

Write your child a letter.

You don't have to be a writer. You just have to be honest.

Your Letter to Your Child > You don't need the right words. You need your words.

> Consider writing your child a letter — not necessarily to send, but to put into words what you want them to know. Here are a few things you might include:

> - What you love most about them right now, at this exact age - Something you wish you had done differently - What you hope for them —

not achievements, but experiences; not resumes, but moments - What you want them to know about the divorce that they might not already know - The promise you are making them, here, today > Keep it. Or give it. Either way, write it.

You picked up this book. That means something. You read children's voices talking about the things they carry, and you stayed with them.

Now do something with it.

Your child is waiting — not necessarily consciously, not always with patience — for evidence that their dad is paying attention. Be that evidence. Today. In something small and consistent and unmistakably yours.

That's the whole thing. That's what this was all about.

Acknowledgments

This book grew out of conversations — some I've had out loud, and many I've had only with myself in the years since my own divorce. To the dads who read The Present Dad and reached out with their stories, their questions, and their honesty: you are in these pages, even where you can't find your name.

To my children, who teach me something new about presence every single week: everything I write is, in the end, a letter to you.

To Laure — for the steadiness you bring to our family and for reminding me, on the days I needed it most, that showing up imperfectly is still showing up.

To the families who trusted me with the hardest parts of their experience so that other families might benefit: your courage is the backbone of this book. The composite voices in these chapters carry real weight because you allowed them to.

To the team at Next Chapter Imprint — thank you for believing that fatherhood is a subject worth taking seriously.

And to every dad holding this book because he wanted to hear what his children might not yet know how to say: that instinct alone tells me your kids are going to be okay.

About the Author

Brandon Antoni is an attorney based in Queen Creek, Arizona, and the author of The Present Dad and The Present Dad Workbook — the first two books in The Present Dad Series. He writes and speaks about fatherhood, divorce, and what it means to stay present in a child's life through the most disorienting chapters of your own.

Brandon is a divorced father of two — a daughter and a son — and is engaged to be married, navigating the rewarding and complicated work of building a blended family. He brings both professional insight and hard-won personal experience to everything he writes.

His work is for dads who are determined to show up — not perfectly, but genuinely — for the children who are counting on them.

He lives in Queen Creek, Arizona.

Continue the Journey

The Present Dad Series

In Their Own Voices is Book 3 of 5 in The Present Dad Series — a complete guide for divorced fathers who are committed to showing up, healing up, and building something lasting with their kids. Each book stands on its own. Together, they cover the full arc of the journey.

Book 1: The Present Dad

~18,800 words | 12 chapters The foundation of the series. An honest, practical guide for divorced dads who want to show up for their children and lead with love — even when life is a mess. Covers showing up with steady love, listening with intention, building stability, integrity, patience, and the daily practice of being present. Start here.

Book 2: The Present Dad Workbook

~9,800 words | 12 chapters The hands-on companion to Book 1. Filled with guided prompts, journaling space, and practical exercises that bring each chapter of The Present Dad into your real life. If you want structure, accountability, and a place to put your thoughts on paper, this is the book that makes the work concrete. The Reflection Questions in In Their Own Voices map directly to exercises in this Workbook.

Book 3: In Their Own Voices: Kids on Divorce and Why Dad Matters

This book.

Seven chapters. Thirty-eight composite voices. The kids in your life have things they haven't said out loud. This book gives them language — and gives you a window into what they're carrying. Read it, then go home different.

Book 4: The Dating Dad

~15,700 words | 11 chapters For when you're ready to think about connection again -- done with integrity and with your children at the center. Covers timing, introductions, navigating your kids' reactions, and what it means to lead with presence in a new relationship. Honest, direct, and written for dads who refuse to let dating become another way of disappearing.

Book 5: The Blended Dad: Shepherding Two Families into One

~24,100 words | 12 chapters The most comprehensive book in the series. For dads further down the road who are building something new -- a blended household, new dynamics, new relationships -- and want to do it with grace. Covers stepparenting, co-parenting across blended systems, loyalty conflicts, and what it means to shepherd two families toward something whole. The road ahead is complicated. This book is for it.

All five books are available through Next Chapter Imprint wherever books are sold. For speaking inquiries, media requests, or to join The Present Dad community, visit thepresentdadseries.com or contact Next Chapter Imprint directly.

Visit thepresentdadseries.com

Follow The Present Dad Project on Facebook

www.ingramcontent.com/pod-product-compliance
Lightning Source LLC
LaVergne TN
LVHW011048110826
845149LV00015B/3405

* 9 7 8 1 9 6 9 5 5 2 0 8 3 *